Marine Mammals

ANIMAL FACTS

by Heather C. Hudak

WEIGL PUBLISHERS INC.

Published by Weigl Publishers Inc.
350 5th Avenue, Suite 3304, PMB 6G
New York, NY 10118-0069 USA
Web site: www.weigl.com

Copyright 2005 WEIGL PUBLISHERS INC.
All rights reserved. No part of this publication may be reproduced, stored
in a retrieval system, or transmitted in any form or by any means, electronic,
mechanical, photocopying, recording, or otherwise, without the prior written
permission of the publisher.

Library of Congress Cataloging-in-Publication Data

Hudak, Heather C., 1975-
  Marine mammals / Heather C. Hudak.
     p. cm. -- (Animal facts)
  Includes bibliographical references (p.   ).
  ISBN 1-59036-201-2 (lib. bdg. : alk. paper) 1-59036-247-0 (softcover)
1. Marine mammals--Juvenile literature. I. Title.
  QL713.2.H84 2004
  599.5--dc22
                              2004001995

Printed in the United States of America
1 2 3 4 5 6 7 8 9 0   08 07 06 05 04

Project Coordinator Heather C. Hudak **Substantive Editor** Tina Schwartzenberger
Copy Editor Donald Wells **Design** Janine Vangool
Layout Bryan Pezzi **Photo Researcher** Ellen Bryan

Photograph and Text Credits
Every reasonable effort has been made to trace ownership and to obtain
permission to reprint copyright material. The publishers would be pleased
to have any errors or omissions brought to their attention so that they may
be corrected in subsequent printings.

Cover: Corel Corporation; **Phillip Colla/www.oceanlight.com:** pages 12, 19L; **Corel Corporation:** pages 1, 7M, 9, 14T, 20; **Digital Stock:** pages 3, 4, 6T, 7T, 11L, 15B, 22; **DigitalVision:** pages 18, 19R, 21; **Photos.com:** pages 5, 7B, 11R, 15T, 17T, 23; **Tom Stack & Associates:** pages 8 (Leonard Lee Rue III), 10 (Tom & Therisa Stack), 13 (Thomas Kitchin); **J. D. Taylor:** pages 6B, 14B, 17B; **U.S. Fish & Wildlife Service:** page 16.

All of the Internet URLs given in the book were valid at the time of publication.
However, due to the dynamic nature of the Internet, some addresses may have
changed, or sites may have ceased to exist since publication. While the author
and publisher regret any inconvenience this may cause readers, no responsibility
for any such changes can be accepted by either the author or the publisher.

Contents

What Is a Marine Mammal? 4

Model Marine Mammals 6

Marine Mammal Markings 8

Marine Mammal Memoirs 10

Life Cycle 12

Marine Mammal Manors 14

Marine Mammal Meals 16

Threatened Marine Mammals 18

Activities 20

Quiz 22

Further Reading/Web Sites 23

Glossary/Index 24

What Is a Marine Mammal?

Manatees are also known as sea cows because they graze on marine grasses and other water plants.

Mammals are warm-blooded animals. They have hair or fur and breathe air through lungs. Mammals give birth to live babies. These animals **nurse** their babies with milk that their bodies produce.

Most mammals live on land. Some live in the water. Marine mammals live in the ocean. A thick layer of **blubber** keeps them warm in cold waters. Marine mammals can remain under water for long periods of time. They come to the surface of the water to breathe air. Marine mammals have **streamlined** bodies to help them swim faster.

Marine mammals have lived on Earth for millions of years. Today, there are more than 115 marine mammal **species**. Each marine mammal has special features. These features help them to survive in different climates and **habitats**.

Sea otters live in the northern Pacific Ocean.

Fast Facts

Most marine mammals do not live in fresh water. They live in salt water, such as oceans. Otters and river dolphins are two mammals that have **adapted** to live in fresh water.

The blue whale is the largest mammal in the world.

Marine mammals store extra oxygen in their muscles and blood. This allows them to stay under water for several minutes without coming up for air.

Sea otters are the smallest marine mammals.

Fish move their tails from side to side to swim. Marine mammals move their tails up and down.

Model Marine Mammals

There are three main groups of marine mammals. These groups are *pinnipeds*, *cetaceans*, and *sirenians*. The *ursidae* and *mustelidae* families each have one species of marine mammal, too.

Pinnipeds are flipper-footed marine mammals. This means they have front and hind, or back, flippers. Sea lions, seals, and walruses are pinnipeds. Pinnipeds live in the ocean, but they can also live on land for long periods of time. They rest, mate, and give birth on land. There are about thirty-three pinniped species on Earth. The California sea lion, pictured left, is a pinniped.

Cetaceans have a streamlined body. They have front flippers and a pair of **flukes**. Cetaceans have a **blowhole** on their backs. Whales, dolphins, and porpoises are cetaceans. There are more than seventy-six species of cetaceans on Earth. The dolphins, pictured here, are cetaceans.

Sirenians have front flippers and large, flat tails. Sirenians are herbivores. This means they eat plants. Manatees, such as the one pictured here, and dugongs are sirenians. They live in warm, tropical waters.

Ursidae are bears. Ursidae have large bodies. They have short, strong limbs and short tails. The polar bear is a member of the ursidae family. It is also a marine mammal. Polar bears spend most of their lives in the water. They rarely come on land. The polar bear, pictured here, is an ursidae.

Mustelidae are members of the weasel family. Sea otters belong to the mustelidae family. Sea otters are furry mammals that spend most of their time in the water. They eat, sleep, and give birth in the water. The sea otter pictured on the left is a mustelidae.

Marine Mammal Markings

Mammals have three basic body features. Mammals have skin and hair or fur. They have internal organ systems, such as the heart and blood cells, the brain, lungs, and stomach. A skeleton protects their vital organs.

All marine mammals share some special body features. These features allow marine mammals to live under water. For example, marine mammals have more blood than land mammals. They can direct their blood flow to their vital organs. This allows marine mammals to slow down their heartbeat and use less oxygen.

Some marine mammals have unique body features. Polar bears and sea otters have thick fur. This fur is made of hollow hairs. These hairs trap cold air and keep the animal warm in cold waters.

Walruses use their tusks as hooks for climbing on the ice in the arctic regions where they live.

Sea lions, fur seals, and walruses are pinnipeds. They can rotate their hind flippers and walk on all four flippers. Walruses have **tusks**. Tusks protect the walrus from polar bear and orca, or killer whale, attacks. Walruses also have two large air sacs on each side of their neck. They fill these sacs with air so their heads will float above the water while they sleep. True, or earless, seals cannot rotate their flippers. They use their large, fan-like hind flippers to move through the water.

Toothed whales have teeth. They also breathe through a single blowhole. Dolphins, porpoises, orca, narwhal, and beluga whales are toothed whales.

Baleen whales do not have teeth. They have rows of horn-like material, called baleen, hanging from the upper jaws of their mouths. Baleens **filter** small fish and small animals, as well as plants called plankton. Whales swallow these foods whole. Baleen whales breathe through two blowholes.

Polar bears have black skin under their white fur.

Fast Facts

Polar bears have large, furry feet. Large feet help spread the bear's weight evenly. This keeps the bear from falling through the thin ice that covers arctic waters.

Marine mammals have excellent underwater vision. This makes finding **prey** easier.

Marine Mammal Memoirs

Scientists use fossils to learn about animal history. There are few marine mammal fossils. This means scientists know very little about the history of marine mammals.

Ancient animals that looked like cows and pigs adapted to ocean life more than 50 million years ago. These animals fed along sea banks. Some began feeding in the water. Their bodies changed over time. Their **limbs** became flippers. New body parts, such as fins and flukes, developed. This made it easier for them to move through the water.

Fossils show scientists that otter-like mammals lived in the area known as Wyoming during the Eocene period 55 to 38 million years ago.

Whales and dolphins adapted from *archaeocetes*. Archaeocetes are similar to hoofed animals, such as cows, camels, and hippopotamuses. This animal group is now **extinct**. Scientists believe true seals adapted from animals that were similar to otters. Eared seals adapted from bear-like animals. Dugongs are related to modern elephants and aardvarks.

Sea otters do not have a layer of blubber. Instead, air trapped inside their fur keeps them warm.

Fast Facts

Cetaceans and sirenians spend their entire lives in the water. They never come on land.

Sea otters are the most recent mammal to adapt to marine life. They adapted from the *enhydritherium* about 5 to 7 million years ago.

Orcas are sometimes called killer whales. However, orcas belong to the dolphin family of cetaceans.

Life Cycle

Female blue whales give birth once every 2 or 3 years. Blue whale calves stay with their mothers for about 1 year.

Marine mammals do not hatch from eggs. Female mammals have eggs. Male mammals **fertilize** an egg inside the female's body. This is called mating. Mammals grow their young inside their bodies. Like land mammals, marine mammals are born live. Female mammals produce milk to feed their young. Over time, they **wean** their young. Young marine mammals learn to survive on their own. Mature marine mammals mate to produce young.

Female whales grow their unborn young inside their bodies for 9 to 16 months. Usually, they give birth to a single calf. The calf swims to the surface for its first breath of air. The young whale is weaned when it is 8 months to 2 years of age. The whale is mature at 6 to 13 years of age. This means it is able to mate. Whales live between 30 and 80 years.

Stellar sea lions mate from mid-May to mid-July each year. They carry their young for about 1 year. Stellar sea lion pups are weaned at about 1 year of age. They can mate when they are about 3 years of age. Stellar sea lions live about 30 years.

Stellar sea lions raise their young in large groups. These groups are called rookeries.

13

Marine Mammal Manors

Marine mammals live in all oceans and seas. Some live in warm waters. Others live in cool waters. Most marine mammals live in salt water. A few dolphin species, such as the Amazon river dolphin, live in fresh water.

Polar bears hunt prey, such as seals, on polar ice floes.

Polar bears live in cold regions. They live in the United States, Canada, Russia, Greenland, and the arctic islands of Norway. They live on pack ice, coastal islands, coastlines, and in arctic waters.

Many beluga whales live near arctic coasts. Some live in large rivers, too.

Cetaceans live in every part of the world. Most large whales travel thousands of miles each year. They live in arctic and antarctic regions in the spring, summer, and autumn. They spend the winter in warm, tropical waters. Bowhead, narwhal, and beluga whales never leave arctic waters.

Sirenians live in warm tropical and subtropical seas. Manatees live in the United States, Central America, South America, the West Indies, and Africa. Manatees have a very thin layer of blubber. This makes it difficult for manatees to stay warm.

Most manatees can become ill if the water is cooler than 70° Fahrenheit (21° Celsius). Florida manatees live in cooler waters during the winter. They gather in the warm springs found in coastal rivers. They also swim to areas where power plants create warm water.

There are about 10,000 Australian sea lions living in nature.

More than 200 manatees gather in the warm water near some power plants during cold weather.

Fast Facts

Sea otters live in the Pacific Ocean. They live in shallow waters and areas with kelp, or seaweed, beds.

Pinnipeds live in oceans and seas in every part of the world.

Marine Mammal Meals

Most marine mammals are carnivores. This means they eat meat. Some eat fish. Others eat squid or shellfish. A few species eat other marine mammals. Polar bears eat seals.

Manatees and dugongs are the only plant-eating marine mammals. Eating plants wears down their teeth often. Manatees have many sets of teeth. These extra teeth replace worn teeth. Manatees live in shallow waters. Here, sunlight can reach water plants better. This causes more plants to grow. This means there is more food for manatees to eat.

Manatees spend 6 to 8 hours each day eating water plants such as hyacinths. Adult manatees need to eat 5 to 10 percent of their body weight each day.

Many marine mammals have adapted to eat certain foods. Most have special body features they use to eat these foods. Sea otters are the only mammals other than humans that use tools to find food. They use rocks to pry prey from their shells. Their diet consists of sea urchins, abalone, mussels, clams, crabs, and snails.

Leopard seals have large mouths. They also have very sharp teeth. This makes it easy for them to catch penguins. They are not fast swimmers, so they must sneak up on their prey. They also eat crabeater seals and a shrimp-like animal called krill.

Crabeater seals have special teeth. Their teeth look like a strainer. They take large gulps of water. Their teeth filter krill from the water.

Bottlenose dolphins have 78 to 96 teeth. Some dolphin species have up to 250 teeth.

Fast Facts

Some bottlenose dolphins work in teams to catch their food. First, they herd fish into a tight group. Then, they take turns catching fish from the group. Dolphins eat fish, but they do not chew. They swallow fish headfirst. This keeps fish spines from catching in their throats.

The only animal that eats leopard seals is the orca.

Threatened Marine Mammals

Animals that are in danger of becoming extinct are called endangered. This means that there are so few of the species that they need protection in order to survive. People are not allowed to hunt endangered animals in the United States.

Oil spills are dangerous for marine mammals. Sea otters and polar bears eat oil when they clean their fur. Seals, whales, and manatees breathe poisonous fumes.

There are many endangered marine mammals. In some cases, their habitat has become too **polluted** and unhealthy. Other habitats have disappeared. Some marine mammals have been overhunted. Others have become entangled in fishers' nets or hurt by boats.

The southern sea otter was once hunted for its fur. Many were killed.

This lowered the sea otter population. Today, the sea otter is protected. It is still in danger from oil spills, which ruin its fur. This causes the otter to become too cold in the water.

Blue whales were once hunted for their blubber and meat.

Construction and pollution destroy places where fish live. This leaves few fish for dolphins to eat.

Tuna fishing nets entangle dolphins. More than 100,000 dolphins died in tuna nets each year in the 1970s and early 1980s. Today, fishers use special methods that will not harm dolphins.

Humans endanger manatees. Manatees swim near the surface of the water. Boats often hit them. This causes broken bones and injuries. Today, there are manatee reserves. These are places where manatees can live free from harm.

Fast Facts

In 2002, an oil spill off the coast of Spain injured or killed thousands of marine mammals and birds.

The Marine Mammal Protection Act was created in 1972. The act protects marine mammals from becoming extinct.

Blue whales are an endangered species. At one time, there were about 200,000 blue whales on Earth. Today, there are about 10,000.

Activities

Blubber Bags

Blubber helps keep marine mammals warm in cool water. The following activity shows how blubber keeps animals warm.

Materials

- ice and water
- bucket
- gloves made from a variety of materials, such as rubber, cotton, wool, or neoprene
- stopwatch
- thermometer
- lard or shortening
- sandwich bags
- tablespoon
- paper towel
- packing tape

1. Scoop a large amount of lard or shortening into a sandwich bag.

2. Turn another sandwich bag inside out. Place this bag inside the bag that is filled with the lard or shortening. Make sure the tops of both bags line up.

3. Use a paper towel to wipe the tops of the bags clean. Then, tape the bags together. Leave a small opening for your hand.

4. Fill the bucket with water. Use the thermometer to measure the water temperature. Add ice until the temperature is between 48 and 64° F (9 and 18° C).

5. Place your bare hand into the ice water. How long can you keep your hand in the water? Repeat the experiment wearing different gloves. Finally, place your hand inside the blubber bag. How long can you keep your hand in the water?

Baby harp seals do not have much blubber. They depend on their mother's milk to keep warm.

Marine Mammal Dangers

Fishing nets and plastic strapping can harm marine mammals. Animals become tangled in strapping and nets. This makes it difficult for them to eat. The following activity shows how garbage harms marine mammals.

Materials

- rubber band
- small pieces of paper
- paper cups

1. Pretend you are a marine mammal. Your hand is the animal's head. Your fingers are its mouth.

2. Lay pieces of paper on a flat surface. Pretend the paper is different types of food. In 10 seconds, use your fingers to pick up as many pieces of paper as possible. Place the paper in the paper cups. How many pieces of food did you catch?

3. Next, wrap the rubber band around your fingers. Be careful not to wrap the rubber band too tightly.

4. In 10 seconds, pick up as many pieces of food as possible using your entangled hand. How many pieces of food did you catch?

5. Did you catch more food with or without the elastic band?

Dolphins caught in fishing nets cannot swim to the surface to breathe.

Quiz

What have you learned about marine mammals? See if you can answer the following questions correctly.

1. How many groups of marine mammals are there?
2. How long have marine mammals lived on Earth?
3. What special body feature do marine mammals have that other mammals do not have?
4. Name three threats to marine mammals.
5. What do marine mammals eat?

Fur seals are known for their thick fur. They may have more than 300,000 hairs per 1 square inch (6.5 square centimeters).

Answers: 1. There are three main groups of marine mammals. 2. Marine mammals have been on Earth for 50 million years. 3. Most marine mammals have blubber. 4. Marine mammals are threatened by pollution, overhunting, oil spills, and becoming tangled in nets. 5. Most marine mammals eat fish, squid, or shellfish.

Further Reading

Field, Nancy and Sally Machlis. *Discovering Marine Mammals*. Middleton, WI: Dog Eared Publications, 2003.

Gowell, Elizabeth Tayntor. *Whales and Dolphins: What They Have in Common*. Washington, DC: Franklin Watts, Incorporated, 2000.

Thomas, Peggy. *Marine Mammal Preservation*. Breckenridge, CO: 21st Century Books, 2000.

Web Sites

To learn about marine mammal research and conservation visit http://nmml.afsc.noaa.gov

Visit The Marine Mammal Center for more information about marine mammals at www.tmmc.org

Polar bears have wide feet to help them swim. The long hair between their toes helps protect their feet from the cold arctic weather.

Glossary

adapted adjusted to different conditions

blowhole an opening used for breathing located on the top of a cetacean's head

blubber layer of fat between the skin and muscles

extinct no longer living any place on Earth

fertilize to make another animal able to produce young

filter a device used to separate items

flukes two limbs that have joined to create a tail

habitats places where animals live in nature

limbs a jointed part of the body, such as an arm or leg

nurse to care for

polluted made unfit or harmful

prey animals that are hunted for food

species type or sort

streamlined designed to move easily through water or air

tusks long, pointed teeth that stick out from the mouth

wean to slowly stop feeding a baby its mother's milk

Index

blubber 5, 11, 14, 19, 20, 22

cetaceans 6, 11, 14

dolphins 5, 6, 9, 11, 14, 17, 19, 21

endangered 18, 19

food 9, 16, 17, 21

habitats 5, 18

life cycle 12, 13

Marine Mammal Protection Act 19
mating 6, 13

pinnipeds 6, 9, 15
polar bears 7, 8, 9, 14, 16, 18, 23

sea otters 5, 7, 8, 11, 15, 17, 18, 19
sirenians 6, 7, 11, 14
stellar sea lions 13

whales 5, 6, 9, 11, 12, 13, 14, 18, 19